Mr. Gizm
Gospel Coloring Book

MW00956092

Spencer Smith

ISBN: 9798841247104

This book is dedicated to my children: Sweet Savannah, Chubbs, Boogies, and Sweet Cakes. My desire is for you to all grow up to be faithful, functional, and fruitful Christians. Your Daddy loves you all so very much.

missionaryspencersmith.com
thirdadam.com

Atonement for Sin

ATONEMENT:

to reconcile two parties that were once enemies

Sinful man is the enemy of God.

The substutionary death of Christ on the cross was the atonement for our sins.

"AND IT CAME TO PASS ON THE MORROW, THAT MOSES SAID UNTO THE PEOPLE, YE HAVE SINNED A GREAT SIN: AND I WILL GO UP UNTO THE LORD: PERADVENTURE I WILL MAKE AN ATONEMENT FOR YOUR SIN." -EXODUS 32:30

"AND NOT ONLY SO, BUT WE ALSO JOY IN GOD THROUGH OUR LORD JESUS CHRIST, BY WHOM WE HAVE NOW RECEIVED THE ATONEMENT." -ROMANS 5:11

Believe on the Lord

BELIEVE:

to be persuaded that something is true based upon the testimony of another

to have full confidence in

to trust

"AND THEY SAID, BELIEVE ON THE LORD JESUS CHRIST,
AND THOU SHALT BE SAVED, AND THY HOUSE."
-ACTS 16:31

"EVEN THE RIGHTEOUSNESS OF GOD WHICH IS BY FAITH OF
JESUS CHRIST UNTO ALL AND UPON ALL
THEM THAT BELIEVE: FOR THERE IS NO DIFFERENCE."
-ROMANS 3:22

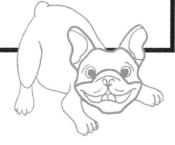

Call

CALL:

to invite

to acknowledge

to appeal to

Christ calls us, and we can call upon Christ.

"FOR WHOSOEVER SHALL CALL UPON THE NAME OF THE
LORD SHALL BE SAVED."
-ROMANS 10:13

"...FOR I AM NOT COME TO CALL THE RIGHTEOUS,
BUT SINNERS TO REPENTANCE."
-MATTHEW 9:13

Day of Christ

DAY OF CHRIST:

the day when Jesus returns to earth to begin his earthly kingdom

Those who are saved will rejoice! Those who are not saved will be sad.

"WHO SHALL ALSO CONFIRM UNTO YOU THE END, THAT YE MAY BE BLAMELESS IN THE DAY OF OUR LORD JESUS CHRIST."
-I CORINTHIANS 1:8

"BEING CONFIDENT OF THIS VERY THING, THAT HE WHICH HATH BEGUN A GOOD WORK IN YOU WILL PERFORM IT UNTIL THE DAY OF JESUS CHRIST."
-PHILIPPIANS 1:6

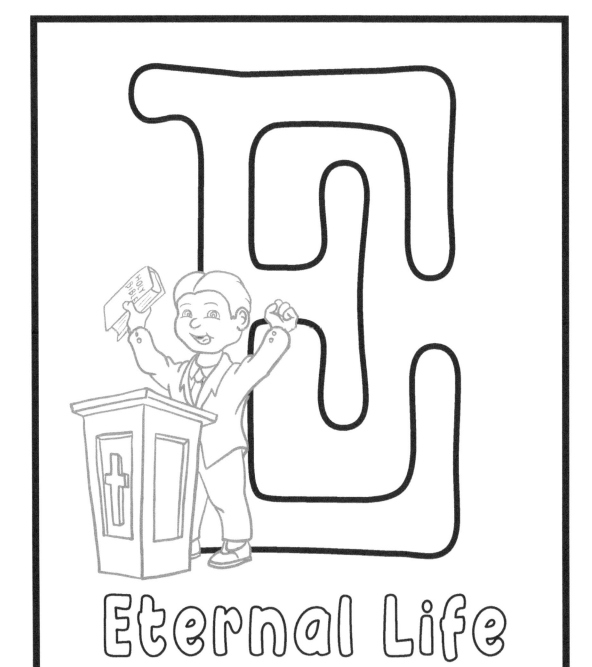

Eternal Life

ETERNAL LIFE:

life with Jesus that will never end for all eternity

Those who receive Christ are granted eternal life.

"...THAT WHOSOEVER BELIEVETH IN HIM SHOULD HAVE EVERLASTING LIFE." -JOHN 3:16

"FOR THE WAGES OF SIN IS DEATH; BUT THE GIFT OF GOD IS ETERNAL LIFE THROUGH JESUS CHRIST OUR LORD." -ROMANS 6:23

"THESE THINGS HAVE I WRITTEN UNTO YOU THAT BELIEVE ON THE NAME OF THE SON OF GOD; THAT YE MAY KNOW THAT YE HAVE ETERNAL LIFE, AND THAT YE MAY BELIEVE ON THE NAME OF THE SON OF GOD." -1 JOHN 5:13

Faith in Christ

FAITH:

confidence in the testimony of God

One who places their faith in Christ believes that Christ has the ability and authority to save them from the penalty of sin.

"THEREFORE BEING JUSTIFIED BY FAITH, WE HAVE PEACE WITH GOD THROUGH OUR LORD JESUS CHRIST."
-ROMANS 5:1

"SO THEN FAITH COMETH BY HEARING, AND HEARING BY THE WORD OF GOD." -ROMANS 10:17

"FOR BY GRACE ARE YE SAVED THROUGH FAITH; AND THAT NOT OF YOURSELVES: IT IS THE GIFT OF GOD.
NOT OF WORKS, LEST ANY MAN SHOULD BOAST."
-EPHESIANS 2:8-9

Grace of God

GRACE:

love and favor with God that is not deserved

a reconciled standing before God

"BEING JUSTIFIED FREELY BY HIS GRACE THROUGH THE REDEMPTION THAT IS IN CHRIST JESUS:" -ROMANS 3:24

"IN WHOM WE HAVE REDEMPTION THROUGH THE BLOOD, THE FORGIVENESS OF SINS, ACCORDING TO THE RICHES OF HIS GRACE." -EPHESIANS 1:7

"FOR BY GRACE ARE YE SAVED THROUGH FAITH; AND THAT NOT OF YOURSELVES; IT IS THE GIFT OF GOD: NOT OF WORKS, LEST ANY MAN SHOULD BOAST." -EPHESIANS 2:8-9

"THAT BEING JUSTIFIED BY HIS GRACE, WE SHOULD BE MADE HEIRS ACCORDING TO THE HOPE OF ETERNAL LIFE." TITUS 3:7

Heaven and Hell

HEAVEN AND HELL:

When you die, you will either go to Heaven or Hell.

All who receive Christ will go to Heaven.
All who reject Christ will go to Hell.

HEAVEN
"AND THE NATIONS OF THEM WHICH ARE SAVED SHALL WALK IN
THE LIGHT OF IT:..." -REVELATION 21:24

"BUT NOW THEY DESIRE A BETTER COUNTRY, THAT IS, AN HEAVENLY:
WHEREFORE GOD IS NOT ASHAMED TO BE CALLED THEIR
GOD: FOR HE HATH PREPARED FOR THEM A CITY."
-HEBREWS 11:16

HELL
"AND WHOSOEVER WAS NOT FOUND WRITTEN IN THE BOOK OF LIFE
WAS CAST INTO THE LAKE OF FIRE."
-REVELATION 20:15

Imputation

IMPUTATION:

the transfer of status from one person to another

Jesus has a righteous standing with God. We do not have a righteous standing with God. When we receive Christ, we have his righteous standing imputed to us.

"AND THE SCRIPTURE WAS FULFILLED WHICH SAITH, ABRAHAM BELIEVED GOD, AND IT WAS IMPUTED UNTO HIM FOR RIGHTEOUSNESS: AND HE WAS CALLED THE FRIEND OF GOD. -JAMES 2:23

"AND BEING FULLY PERSUADED THAT, WHAT HE HAD PROMISED, HE WAS ABLE TO ALSO PERFORM. AND THEREFORE IT WAS IMPUTED TO HIM FOR RIGHTEOUSNESS. -ROMANS 4: 21-22

JUSTIFICATION:

to be declared free from guilt and punishment by a Judge

God is the Judge, and when you are saved, you are declared just by the Great Judge.

"BEING JUSTIFIED FREELY BY HIS GRACE THROUGH THE REDEMPTION THAT IS IN CHRIST JESUS." -ROMANS 3:24

"BUT TO HIM THAT WORKETH NOT, BUT BELIEVETH ON HIM THAT JUSTIFIETH THE UNGODLY, HIS FAITH IS COUNTED FOR RIGHTEOUSNESS." -ROMANS 4:5

"THEREFORE BEING JUSTIFIED BY FAITH, WE HAVE PEACE WITH GOD THROUGH OUR LORD JESUS CHRIST." -ROMANS 5:1

"WHO SHALL LAY ANY THING TO THE CHARGE OF GOD'S ELECT? IT IS GOD THAT JUSTIFIETH." - ROMANS 8:33

Kingdom

KINGDOM:

the inhabitants or population subject to a king

When we are saved, we become citizens of this coming kingdom.

Those who are not saved are not allowed into the coming kingdom.

"FROM THAT TIME JESUS BEGAN TO PREACH, AND TO SAY, REPENT: FOR THE KINGDOM OF HEAVEN IS AT HAND." -MATTHEW 4:17

"WHO HATH DELIVERED US FROM THE POWER OF DARKNESS, AND HATH TRANSLATED US INTO THE KINGDOM OF HIS DEAR SON:" -COLOSSIANS 1:13

"AND THE LORD SHALL DELIVER ME FROM EVERY EVIL WORK, AND WILL PRESERVE ME UNTO HIS HEAVENLY KINGDOM: TO WHOM BE GLORY FOR EVER AND EVER. AMEN." -2 TIMOTHY 4:18

Love of God

LOVE OF GOD:

Love- the deepest form of affection possible

God loves you so much that he gave his Son Jesus to die for your sins.

God's love for us causes us to love him back!

"FOR GOD SO LOVED THE WORLD, THAT HE GAVE HIS ONLY BEGOTTEN SON, THAT WHOSOEVER BELIEVETH IN HIM SHOULD NOT PERISH, BUT HAVE EVERLASTING LIFE." -JOHN 3:16

"BUT GOD COMMENDETH HIS LOVE TOWARD US, IN THAT, WHILE WE WERE YET SINNERS, CHRIST DIED FOR US." -ROMANS 5:8

:AND WALK IN LOVE, AS CHRIST ALSO HATH LOVED US, AND HATH GIVEN HIMSELF FOR US AN OFFERING AND A SACRIFICE TO GOD FOR A SWEETSMELLING SAVOUR." -EPHESIANS 5:2

Doctrine Matters

Mercy of God

MERCY OF GOD:

Mercy- not giving judgment when judgment is deserved

We deserve Judgment, but God has withheld judgment for a time so we can hear the gospel and be saved.

God's mercy holds back his judgment for a time because he loves us and does not want to judge us.

"NOT BY WORKS OF RIGHTEOUSNESS WHICH WE HAVE DONE, BUT ACCORDING TO HIS MERCY HE SAVED US, BY THE WASHING OF REGENERATION, AND RENEWING OF THE HOLY GHOST." -TITUS 3:5

"BLESSED BE THE GOD AND FATHER OF OUR LORD JESUS CHRIST, WHICH ACCORDING TO HIS ABUNDANT MERCY HATH BEGOTTEN US AGAIN UNTO A LIVELY HOPE BY THE RESURRECTION OF JESUS CHRIST FROM THE DEAD," -I PETER 1:3

Name
above all Names

NAME ABOVE ALL NAMES:

The name of Jesus Christ is the highest title to ever be given to anyone.

This name is given to the only one who has the Authority and Ability to declare anyone saved.

Those who will be saved must call upon that name to do so. There is salvation in no other name than Jesus.

"AND SHE SHALL BRING FORTH A SON, AND THOU SHALT CALL HIS NAME JESUS: FOR HE SHALL SAVE HIS PEOPLE FROM THEIR SINS." -MATTHEW 1:21

"NEITHER IS THERE SALVATION IN ANY OTHER: FOR THERE IS NONE OTHER NAME UNDER HEAVEN GIVEN AMONG MEN, WHEREBY WE MUST BE SAVED." -ACTS 4:12

"WHEREFORE GOD ALSO HATH HIGHLY EXALTED HIM, AND GIVEN HIM A NAME WHICH IS ABOVE EVERY NAME: THAT AT THE NAME OF JESUS EVERY KNEE SHOULD BOW, OF THINGS IN HEAVEN, AND THINGS IN EARTH, AND THINGS UNDER THE EARTH; AND THAT EVERY TONGUE SHOULD CONFESS THAT JESUS CHRIST IS LORD, TO THE GLORY OF GOD THE FATHER." -PHILIPPIANS 2:9-11

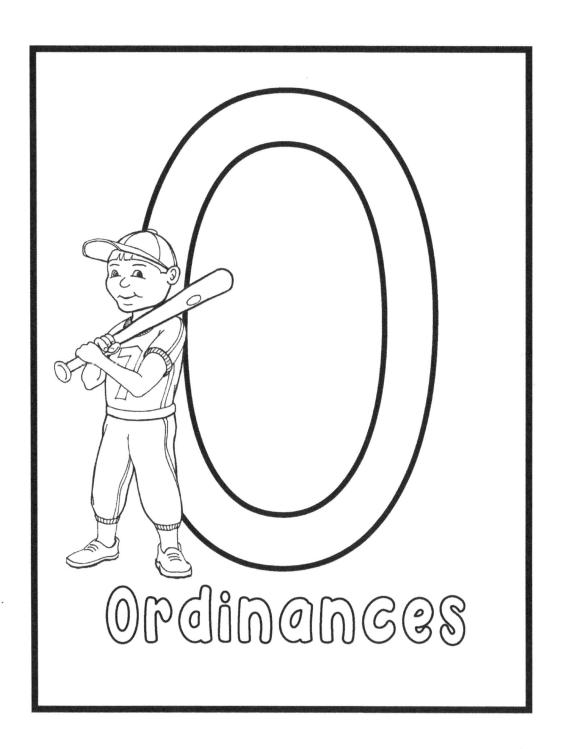

Ordinances

ORDINANCES:

a rule or law put in place by a higher authority
An ordinace is similar to a law or command.
We have broken God's ordinances and deserve punishment.

In Roman government, when someone was crucified, the ordinances
they broke were put into print and nailed to the cross with them
so that everyonewould know of what crime they're being punished.

Jesus took our "handwriting of ordinances" and nailed it to his
cross, thus dying for our crimes and sins.

"AND YOU, BEING DEAD IN YOUR SINS AND THE
UNCIRCUMCISION OF YOUR FLESH, HATH HE
QUICKENED TOGETHER WITH HIM,
HAVING FORGIVEN YOU ALL YOUR TRESPASSES;
BLOTTING OUT THE HANDWRITING OF
ORDINANCES THAT WAS AGAINST US,
AND IT TOOK IT OUT OF THE WAY, NAILING IT TO
HIS CROSS;" -COLOSSIANS 2:13-14

DOCTRINE MATTERS

Peace of God

PEACE:

When two people are at war, the only way to end the conflict is for someone to declare peace.

Before we were saved, we were an enemy of God. God was against us, and we were against God.

Jesus Christ became the means of peace between us and God the Father. Without Jesus, we are still the enemies of God.

"FOR HE IS OUR PEACE, WHO HATH MADE BOTH ONE, AND HATH BROKEN DOWN THE MIDDLE WALL OF PARTITION BETWEEN US; HAVING ABOLISHED IN HIS FLESH THE ENMITY, EVEN THE LAW OF COMMANDMENTS CONTAINED IN ORDINANCES; FOR TO MAKE IN HIMSELF OF TWAIN ONE NEW MAN, SO MAKING PEACE." -EPHESIANS 2:14-15

"AND, HAVING MADE PEACE THROUGH THE BLOOD OF HIS CROSS, BY HIM TO RECONCILE ALL THINGS UNTO HIMSELF, BY HIM, I SAY, WHETHER THEY BE THINGS IN EARTH, OR IN HEAVEN." -COLOSSIANS 1:20

Quickened

QUICKENED:

Quickened is an old English word that means "to be given life." When we were dead in our sins, Jesus quickened us, and gave us spiritual life.

When a radio is not plugged into a wall, it is dead. When plugged into an outlet, it suddenly has life. We were dead until we were "plugged in" to Jesus Christ, then we were given new life.

"EVEN WHEN WERE DEAD IN SINS, HATH QUICKENED US TOGETHER WITH CHRIST, [BY GRACE YE ARE SAVED;]"
-EPHESIANS 2:5

"AND YOU, BEING DEAD IN YOUR SINS AND THE UNCIRCUMCISION OF YOUR FLESH, HATH HE QUICKENED TOGETHER WITH HIM, HAVING FORGIVEN YOU ALL TRESPASSES;"
-COLOSSIANS 2:13

"FOR CHRIST ALSO HATH ONCE SUFFERED FOR SINS, THE JUST FOR THE UNJUST, THAT HE MIGHT BRING US TO GOD, BEING PUT TO DEATH IN THE FLESH, BUT QUICKENED BY THE SPIRIT:" -1 PETER 3:18

Doctrine Matters

Redeemed

REDEEMED:

to be delivered from punishment, bondage, penalty or distress

We were under the penalty of sin, but Jesus redeemed us from that penalty when he shed his blood for us.

"CHRIST HATH REDEEMED US FROM THE CURE OF THE LAW, BEING MADE A CURSE FOR US: FOR IT IS WRITTEN, CURSED IS EVERY ONE THAT HANGETH ON A TREE." -GALATIANS 3:13

"FORASMUCH AS YE KNOW THAT YE WERE NOT REDEEMED WITH CORRUPTIBLE THINGS, AS SILVER AND GOLD, FROM YOUR VAIN CONVERSATION RECEIVED BY TRADITION FROM YOUR FATHERS; BUT WITH THE PRECIOUS BLOOD OF CHRIST, AS OF A LAMB WITHOUT BLEMISH AND WITHOUT SPOT." -1 PETER 1:18-19

Saved from Sin

SAVED:

kept from injury, death, or destruction

We were headed for eternal destruction in Hell, but we were saved by Jesus Christ.

One who has trusted Christ has been saved from the second death in Hell.

"MUCH MORE THEN, BEING NOW JUSTIFIED BY HIS BLOOD, WE SHALL BE SAVED FROM WRATH THROUGH HIM." -ROMANS 5:9

"FOR IF, WHEN WE WERE ENEMIES, WE WERE RECONCILED TO GOD BY THE DEATH OF HIS SON, MUCH MORE, BEING RECONCILED, WE SHALL BE SAVED BY HIS LIFE." -ROMANS 5:10

"NOT BY WORKS OF RIGHTEOUSNESS WHICH WE HAVE DONE, BUT ACCORDING TO HIS MERCY HE SAVED US, BY THE WASHING OF REGENERATION, AND RENEWING OF THE HOLY GHOST;" -TITUS 3:5

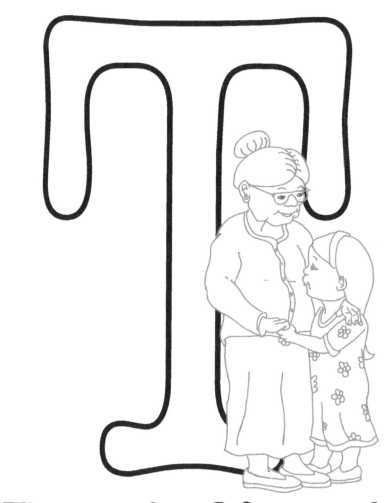

Trust Christ

TRUST:

to rely on another; to believe another

Jesus said that he can save us, and we must rely solely upon Him to be saved. We must trust Christ.

To trust anything else to get us to Heaven will fail.

"IN WHOM YE ALSO TRUSTED, AFTER THAT YE HEARD THE WORD OF TRUTH, THE GOSPEL OF YOUR SALVATION: IN WHOM ALSO AFTER THAT YE BELIEVED, YE WERE SEALED WITH THAT HOLY SPIRIT OF PROMISE," -EPHESIANS 1:13

"FOR THE WHICH CAUSE I ALSO SUFFER THESE THINGS: NEVERTHELESS I AM NOT ASHAMED: FOR I KNOW WHOM I HAVE BELIEVED, AND AM PERSUADED THAT HE IS ABLE TO KEEP THAT WHICH I HAVE COMMITTED UNTO HIM AGAINST THAT DAY." -2 TIMOTHY 1:12

Unbelief

UNBELIEF:

the opposite of belief
refusing to believe the gospel

To choose not to believe the gospel is to make God a liar, which is a terrible sin. Those who refuse to believe the gospel will goto Hell when they die.

"HE THAT BELIEVETH ON HIM IS NOT CONDEMNED: BUT HE THAT BELIEVETH NOT IS CONDEMNED ALREADY, BECAUSE HE HATH NOT BELIEVED IN THE NAME OF THE ONLY BEGOTTEN SON OF GOD." -JOHN 3:18

"AND FOR THIS CAUSE GOD SHALL SEND THEM STRONG DELUSION, THAT THEY SHOULD BELIEVE A LIE: THAT THEY ALL MIGHT BE DAMNED WHO BELIEVE NOT THE TRUTH, BUT HAD PLEASURE IN UNRIGHTEOUSNESS." -2 THESSALONIANS 2:11-12

Victory

VICTORY:

Jesus died and rose again. He won the
victory over the grave.
Those who trust Christ have this
victory as well.

There is victory in Jesus!

"FOR WHATSOEVER IS BORN OF GOD OVERCOMETH THE WORLD;
AND THIS IS THE VICTORY THAT OVERCOMETH
THE WORLD, EVEN OUR FAITH." -1 JOHN 5:4

"SO WHEN THIS CORRUPTIBLE SHALL HAVE PUT ON INCORRUPTION,
AND THIS MORTAL SHALL HAVE PUT ON IMMORTALITY,
THEN SHALL BE BROUGHT TO PASS THE SAYING THAT IS WRITTEN,
DEATH IS SWALLOWED UP IN VICTORY. O DEATH, WHERE
IS THY STING? OH GRAVE, WHERE IS THY VICTORY? THE STING
OF DEATH IS SIN; AND THE STRENGTH OF SIN IS THE LAW.
BUT THANKS BE TO GOD, WHICH GIVETH US THE VICTORY
THROUGH OUR LORD JESUS CHRIST."
-1 CORINTHIANS 15:54-57

Washed

WASHED:

to cleanse; to make clean

We were once dirty in our sins, but Jesus washed us, and made us clean before Him.

"AND SUCH WERE SOME OF YOU: BUT YE ARE WASHED,
BUT YE ARE SANCTIFIED, BUT YE ARE
JUSTIFIED IN THE NAME OF THE LORD JESUS, AND BY
THE SPIRIT OF OUR GOD." -1 CORINTHIANS 6:11

"AND FROM JESUS CHRIST, WHO IS THE FAITHFUL WITNESS
AND THE FIRST BEGOTTEN OF THE DEAD,
AND THE PRINCE OF THE KINGS OF THE EARTH. UNTO
HIM THAT LOVED US, AND WASHED US FROM OUR SINS IN HIS
OWN BLOOD." -REVELATION 1:5

Zealous

ZEALOUS:

To work in an excited and energetic way. To be excited about a cause.

We should be excited about our salvation in Christ, and our desire to tell others about Jesus.

Jesus should make us go and tell the world!

"For I know the forwardness of your mind, for which I boast of you to them of Macedonia, that Achaia was ready a year ago; and your zeal hath provoked very many."
- 2 Corinthians 9:2

"Who gave himself for us, that he might redeem us from all iniquity, and purify unto himself a peculiar people, zealous of good works.." -Titus 2:14

Rejoice Evermore

1 Thessalonians 5:16

For by Grace are ye Saved

Ephesians 2:8

Believe on the Lord Jesus Christ
Acts 16:31

HELP MR. GIZMO FIND HIS WAY TO THE BIBLE!!!

Trust in the Lord with all thine Heart
Proverbs 3:5

Ye are the Light of the World
Matthew 5:14

Connect The Dots To Draw Gizmo

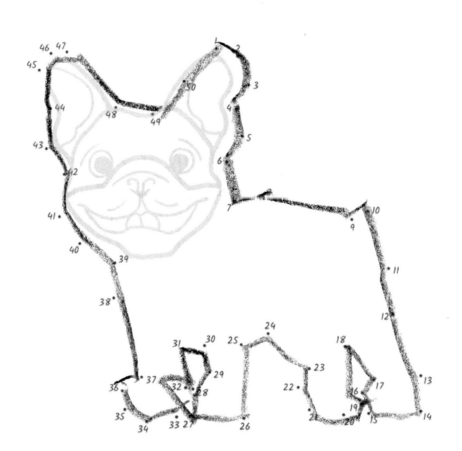

Children, Obey your Parents in the Lord, for this is Right

Ephesians 6:1

Help Mr. Gizmo Find The Bible!!!!

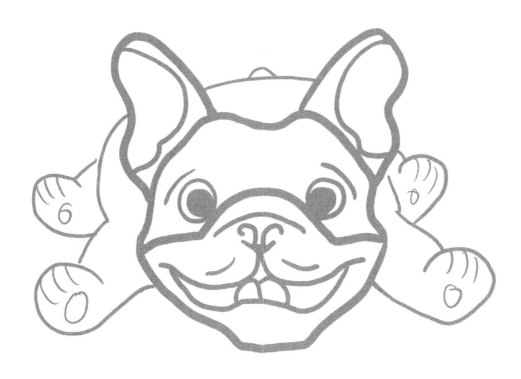

A Soft Answer Turneth Away Wrath

Proverbs 15:1

Delight thyself also in the Lord
Psalms 37:4

Make a Joyful Noise unto the Lord
Psalms 98:4

Connect The Dots To Draw Gizmo

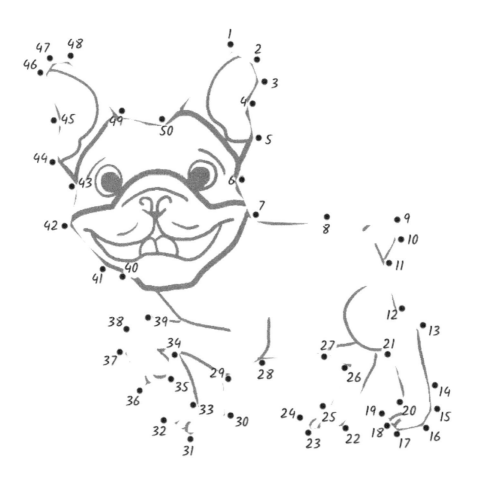

No Man can Serve Two Masters

Matthew 6:24

O Give Thanks unto the Lord,

for He is GoOd

Psalms 136:1

Quench Not the Spirit

1 Thessalonians 5:19

I will Praise thee with my Whole Heart

Psalms 138:1

**What Time I am Afraid,
I Will Trust in Thee**

Psalms 56:3

For Whosoever Shall Call upon the Name of the Lord Shall be Saved

Romans 10:13

Pray Without Ceasing

1 Thessalonians 5:17

Let All Things be Done with Charity
Corinthians 16:14

Be ye Kind One to Another
Ephesians 4:32

Help Mr. Gizmo Find The Bible!!!

Pray Without Ceasing

1 Thessalonians 5:17

Let All Things be Done with Charity

Corinthians 16:14

Be ye Kind One to Another
Ephesians 4:32

Help Mr. Gizmo Find The Bible!!!

Set your Affection on Things Above, Not on Things on the Earth
Colossians 3:2

Commit thy Works unto the LORD
Proverbs 16:3

In all thy Ways Acknowledge Him,
and He Shall Direct thy Path

Proverbs 3:6

Keep thy Heart with all Diligence

Proverbs 4:23

For we Walk by Faith, not by Sight
2 Corinthians 5:7

If Sinners Entice thee, Consent thou Not
Proverbs 1:10

Let No Man Despise thy Youth

1 Timothy 4:12

But my God shall Supply all your
Need According to His Riches in Glory

Phillippians 4:19

Love thy Neighbor as Thyself

Matthew 22:39

Godliness with Contentment is Great Gain
1 Timothy 6:6

Do all Things without Murmurings and Disputes
Philippians 2:14

For ye are Bought with a Price

1 Corinthians 6:20

Sing unto the Lord a New Song

Psalms 98:1

Be Strong and of a Good Courage

Joshua 1:9

But be ye Doers of the Word

James 1:22

For God so Loved the World

John 3:16

I can do all Things through Christ which Strengtheneth me

Phillippians 4:13

Put on the Whole Armour of God,
that ye may be ble to Stand
Against the Wiles of the Devil
Ephesians 6:11

Made in the USA
Monee, IL
24 November 2024

71109723R00057